Plant Arrangements

Plant arrangements are made of (flowering and foliage) plants, botanical and artificial materials. They are planted or arranged in one or several containers by means of a supporting medium. Various techniques are applied, according to the specific needs of the material and the emotions you want to express with your arrangement. Water is an essential element for most botanical materials used in a plant arrangement.

Per, Max and Tomas

Creativity with flowers

Plant Arrangements

Per Benjamin
Max van de Sluis
Tomas De Bruyne

stichting
kunstboek

Plants and plant arrangements sold on a town square mid 18th century.

The history of plant arrangements

Flowers and plants, appreciated for their beauty, medicinal use, as flavouring in our cookery and used as a means of expression, are part of the whole history of human existence. Since Man first settled and built homes, flowers have been used as decoration, for celebrations and as offerings, from single blooms to much more advanced works. The need to decorate and make our homes more beautiful, to bring part of the natural world that is so important to us inside, has always been part of our lives. Historically they have been used by religions in temples and churches, by royalty to demonstrate their power and, amongst the rich, often as sheer amusement. Messages from gods, priests, kings and poets. Originally it all started with Man settling down and starting to farm the land, gathering those plants needed for food and a few for their beauty, in fields, gardens and eventually pots. Extensive evidence of flower use from ancient times is to be found in simple wall paintings, murals, and, in more recent times, on mosaics, frescos on artefacts and described in writings and paintings. Plant arrangements in earlier ages consisted mostly of single plants, smaller and bigger trees planted in containers, placed in gardens and patios of palaces and temples. From these garden pots with plants and trees it is a long journey to today's use of plants in and outside the house. As with our ancestors, the more exotic the more interesting. To show the evolution of plants and plant arrangements, the various fields of usage, techniques and styles, we take you on a personal journey through history that will give reason and insight as well as inspiration.

We can trace plant arrangements or potted plants back to Mesopotamian kingdoms, some 6000 BC, between the Euphrates and the Tigris, today's Iraq, where priests and kings ruled. Fantastic palaces and temples were erected in honour of earthly and heavenly powers, all decorated with flowers and plants of all sorts made by skilled gardeners/florists. From wall paintings and murals we can see how richly such places were decorated. Most famous were the hanging gardens of Babylon, one of the world wonders at the time. This was an artificially created garden on several levels with an intricate watering system. Given by the king to his wife, to resemble the home country of the queen, to compensate her longing for home. Artificial flowerbeds and lots of containers and pots were used to host all the plants brought in from all around this part of the world. We see planted alleys, bigger pots with both plants and trees of all variations. Popular amongst many were all kinds of palms, citrus, figs and many blooming plants. In general, the gardens hold a mix of purely decorative plants and household orientated ones. Fruit, leaves and herbs important for culinary and religious use are cultivated.

From ancient Egypt we have more evidence of the importance of flowers as decoration as well as the techniques and the actual materials used. Evidence from paintings as well as actual dried preserved flower works, more than 4000 years old, which still show the strong colours used. Plants and plant arrangements sorted by gardeners, who created cut flower works as well. There were strict plans on how gardens should look and fashion decided what plants were popular. But the unquestionable number one was the water lily, the holy flower of the Nile and symbol of Ra, the god of the sun. These were grown in ponds as well as bigger pots filled with water, often with Papyrus, another very important plant to Egyptians. More common trees, plants and flowers were, palms, olive, fig, citrus, pomegranate, papyrus, chrysanthemum, roses, poppies, larkspur, corn flower and many herbs. An interesting fact is that, together with the flowers, fruits and vegetables were used. Temples and palaces were richly decorated and fantastic gardens including ponds and plenty of potted plants were created to show status in society as well as godly powers.

The most common plants in old Egypt: Papyrus and Water Lilly.

We see the same use of flowers in Greece, where each god had their own symbol from nature. This explains our use of some of those materials today! The Goddess of love, Aphrodite, had white and red roses as her symbol; the god of the dead, Hades, had cypress while his wife, Persephone, goddess of the dead, had white lilies. The god of fertility, wine and celebration, Dionysus, had vine and ivy leaves, the god of matrimony, Hymenaios, had myrtle. When towns like Athens expanded, many of these plants were potted and placed in courtyards and other open spaces where lack of actual soil to grow occurred. This is how many of our plants started to find their way into our homes! This was also the fashion in town squares and in front of important public buildings and temples. Plants and flowers were now commonly sold on town markets. Later, when flowers were commonly cultivated and with new flowers and traditions brought in from Persia by Alexander the Great, people started decorating their homes and tables with both plant and floral arrangements, garlands and wreaths. Flowers held an important position as means of communication; a small wreath of olive leaves on the door signalled a boy's birth, violets a girl's and cypress on the door, death in the family. After a party, boys used wreaths as a symbol of their love, hanging it on the door of their girl's family's house! All of this unspoken language needed lots of foliage and flowers, so better to have them at hand in pots around the house.

Rome followed the Greek traditions, and, taking the rose to its heart, made it the flower of the empire. Apart from the rose, many other flowers such as lilacs, lilies, citrus, anemones, daffodils, stocks, all kind of herbs were used both for their good scents and colours. On many murals and mosaics from the time we see the most exquisite gardens, with balustrades topped with decorative pots filled with beautiful plants, bigger ones on the floor of the terraces. For the rich, having a garden in their town home was a sign of luxury, stating their position and rank, as well as a place to hide from city life, surrounded by green, flowers and scents. Rome, at its peek of power, was a city with over one million inhabitants, far away from nature, so flowers and plants were sold on all major markets in the city. Around the city, Campana flowers and plants were grown both in fields and in greenhouses. These greenhouses, the forerunners of today's glass houses, were made from semi transparent sheets and heated with a system of hot water channels, just to provide the city with flowers, fruits, vegetables and plants all year round. The Romans also believed in the curative properties of plants as well as their spiritual power, keeping them as potted plants as well as making wreaths from different herbs for their doors to protect homes from evil spirits. Most flower and plant traditions were old pagan ones, but slowly we see a change with the coming of the new Christian religion.

The Middle Ages saw the battle of the flowers! With Christianity, many traditions were abolished as being pagan, but those concerning flowers were impossible to stop. Not being able to ban flower use, the church changed and made flowers their own. Flower symbolism was changed to suit the Christian message; flower use was christened! The rose, the symbol of Rome, became the most important symbol for the church, the white rose for Virgin Mary and the red one for Christ. Usage was more moderate and they were not used as offerings but purely for decorative use. And most used and affordable were potted plants of all variations. We see potted plants take the step into our homes, ending up on balconies, balustrades and front patios. During most of the Middle Ages flower use decreased because of constant strains on people due to wars, disease and poverty, but the tradition was kept alive by the monasteries, in walled secluded gardens. In monasteries, flowers and plants were grown and kept for their medical use mainly, but also for pure beauty. From tapestries of the time we also know that flowers, plants and vase arrangements were used in royal courts around Europe. Here and among the rich, money was still spent on flowers and plants and then, later in the Middle Ages, once again started spreading down through the layers of society. The profession was under pressure but at the end of the period flowers and flower works were once again sold in markets and the professionals gathered in guilds around central Europe, like the *Chapelier des fleurs* in Paris.

With the Renaissance came the rebirth of science, humanities and arts in general, and the focus changed from heaven to earth. Flower design flourished again. There are descriptions of huge Renaissance dinner parties, with everything but flowers well described. We simply have to presume they used plenty of flowers. From evidence, we know that decorations were getting more elaborate. They had miniature gardens

Entrance decorated with plants.

Renaissance plant arrangement.

complete with hedges, flower fields, fountains and statues, complemented with wreaths, garlands and flower petals. These petals on the tables were the forerunners to our stitched and printed tablecloths. These miniature gardens were inspired by the ones outside, and especially influenced by the monastery gardens. The fashion was to divide the garden design in four, each part signifying either one of the four directions or one of the four known continents, and to have a fountain in the centre. Here we see a mixed use of plants. Decorating with flowers and plants became affordable and more common in normal homes because of the new way of furnishing homes with tables and cabinets. That often consisted of the simple potted plant on the windowsill or in the backyard, bringing nature into city homes. Commonly used were all kinds of bulbs, herbs and, with plants, myrtle, ivy, buxus, citrus, vines and roses were popular.

With the discovery of new continents during the 1600's and early 1700's Baroque and Rococo periods, new flowers appeared in Europe, making botanics fashionable and creating a couple of flower trends. Passionate trends raged in colonial countries like France, Belgium, Holland and England. New Chinese roses, peonies, orchids from South America, bulbs like fritillaries, hyacinth from Middle Asia became massive. The famous 'tulip mania' speculation made the tulip ridiculously expensive. But behind the speculation was a genuine interest for botany and nature. Plants, as roots and as seeds were brought and then grown and cared for in glass houses, orangeries and private botanical gardens owned by rich merchants. It was in one of these, Carolus Linnaeus, the father of today's botanical nomenclature, first got to see many foreign and exotic plants.

Gardeners planning and planting.

During the Baroque period, the "masculine" more pompous and darker of the two, the style was rich in materials and colours, for showing wealth, often using accessories like new tropical fruits, exotic birds, butterflies and other rare things. Always centred on plants and flowers, usually potted, treated as precious jewellery. These were only for the very rich in society. Most common and from where we have learnt much about the arrangements of these times, were paintings of flower pieces. These "flower-paintings" from artists like Ambrosius Bosschaert and Johann Knapp were the fashion of the time. Often showing well-known flowers, mixing seasons as well as continents, other than really accurately copying a flower arrangement, but they give a good idea of the actual ones!

Everything was blooming in the 1700's! The French court was the trendsetter of Europe and at the era of Rococo and Rousseau, the longing for nature made them turn their great rooms into actual natural landscapes for parties. Flowers were the thing for all decorations for celebrations: hanging from the ceiling, on walls, in decorations on table-cloths as well as on clothes, both on men and women, wallpaper, ceramics, cutlery…everything was blooming! Popular flowers were sweet peas, roses, freesias, lilacs and hyacinths, all appreciated for their scents and more feminine look. If you could not afford actual flowers, artificial ones were made out of paper or fabric, a hobby for many women, rich and poor.

Stately home decorated according to fashion.

Up until now, what we call 'plant arrangement' and potted plants had been something for the absolute top layer of society, religious and earthly powers, priests, kings and their entourages. They were the ones with the power and money, using flowers as offerings, decoration for sacred celebrations, enjoyment and to show off their power. But now came a change with new popular plants, plants being easy to propagate; from seeds, side shoots or cuttings, being shared amongst friends and passed on in families.

Glasshouse hanging on a windowsill.

Fashionably decorated home with a great diversity of plants.

Geranium, much appreciated for its blooms and an easy plant to multiply with shoots.

During the first half of the 1800's, during the Empire period and later Biedermeier époque, and mass industrialization, flower handicraft took big steps forward. More energy was put into decorating homes with real flowers. Flowers now became more easily accessible in markets and in the newly opened flower shops in all major cities around Europe. The first known flower shop was opened in Paris by a Madame Prevost. She and her two employees became famous for their bouquets and arrangements and probably plants as well.

We saw the status of the profession rising with the development of works and skills. There was a new style, once again from France, this time with Napoleon Bonaparte as trendsetter of the Empire style. A stricter style inspired from ancient Egypt and Rome, with darker fabrics on furniture and draped around windows. The new trendy thing all over Europe was plants of all kinds, preferably palms, room Picea, Ficus, Fuchsia, Azalea and cacti on special 'flower tables', pedestals and in huge pots. Literally small jungles were created inside living rooms and other public spaces. Rare plants such as orchids, Camellias, ferns etc were grown in special glasshouses attached outside of the windowsill or placed inside. In many European countries, and especially in England, we see special clubs being created around flowers and plants, often focusing on one single variety, such as Saintpaulia, Azalea, orchids, etc. With growing interest, interbreeding, focus on sturdiness, flower size and more, we see a rapid change towards better quality plants, much more like today's pot plants. Before this era, most of us would hardly recognize the plants, many being thin, rickety, with small and few flowers.

Outside the cities flower use spread to the commoners and farmers. In their windows appeared Geranium, cacti, Begonia, myrtle and the now affordable bulbs. The latter often grown in special glasses with water underneath. Cared for and passed on between generations and to friends.

In the latter part of the 1800's, the Romantic period, flowering and more romantic plants, as the name signifies, were popular. A natural and open look, both domestic and exotic, inspired by gardens and nature were the highest fashion, especially in Victorian England. We see glasshouses and the wealthy built winter gardens and orangeries to host their most precious plants. The fashion was to grow and propagate out of season plants, herbs and fruits. Nothing better than flowering Lilies of the Valley, azaleas and strawberries on a winter dinner table. So normal for us today that we don't think about it, but difficult and very expensive at the time.

Flowers and plants were given and grown to express emotions, often those difficult to say upfront or simply to enhance the message. Many books were written on the subject, often conflicting and overlapping each other! Some of the more common flowers and meanings were;
- Violets – take me with you!
- Lily of the valley – quietly I have long adored you!
- Narcissus – you are too self-complacent!
- Box – my faithfulness is forever!
- Nettle – how can you be so cruel?

One can easily imagine the complexity of these arrangements and of love!

Myrtle – symbol of love and a must in wedding bouquets. These plants were treated with extra care. Usually a newborn girl got her plant and then she was supposed to care for this until her wedding, using her own myrtle, and finally passing it on to her daughters.

Special flower works were being produced for specific events, weddings and holidays like Christmas and Easter; there was a feeling of pride and belief in the future. A wider selection with better quality was now available thanks to better growing techniques and imports from the Italian and French Riviera. Proper education for florists started, exhibitions and competitions strengthened and developed the profession. Plants and even more so flowers were becoming an affordable luxury to people of all classes.

We now see advanced, time-consuming, technically well-done works built from scratch, making the florist a carpenter as well as a florist, designs in the shape of crowns, birds, musical instruments, chandeliers and many more! Dry works were mostly built on a base of clay; others consisted of tightly packed wired moss on wood or metal structures, with flower heads and foliage arranged in a tight decorative manner. Besides these 'special' decorations, wreaths, garlands and bouquets were still the most common and affordable works for the masses.

When baskets were fashionable, especially the famous Elisa basket, they were either lined with waxed waterproof paper or fitted with customized metal containers, and then a preferred medium was inserted and soaked. The designs were either more open, with flowers facing both directions, or more static with an obvious backside and the flowers facing forward. There were a lot of discussions concerning basket design and whether or not the flowers should exceed the height limit of the top handle.

Plant arrangement with Convallaria

Plant arrangement with ribbons.

And then to top off the whole creation, often a big bow was added on the handle, trailing down through the flowers, ending with another one on the side of the basket. We also saw the start of plant decoration of either mixed or single variations preferably in a basket and decorated with ribbons. Popular were Azaleas, Begonias and, in winter, Christmas rose and Lily of the Valley. Not much changed in the first half of the 20th century. Moss, hay and wire were the materials in use, giving all florists at the time black fingers, not green ones! Decorative style was still predominant.

Finally, the 70's, with better education and design concepts instead of simple arranging, saw a rapid change and diversification into different styles: Formal linear and Vegetative styles. Formal linear, the first style to overtake the Decorative one is, as the name suggests, all about forms of blooms and foliage and lines of stems and branches. With the search for contrasts as a crucial element.
Contrasts in materials, textures and, most significantly, in colours made this style totally different. Each single material was important compared to the Decorative style, where volume and total expression were most significant. This opened new possibilities for florists who could use a wider range of designs and materials. The Vegetative style is totally different, taking its inspiration from nature, habitats, seasons and ways of growing. Here we see miniature landscapes and, later, arrangements that resemble the essence of a special season or habitat! What we also see in the 80's and 90's the increased use of twigs, branches and other lines of botanical and artificial kind, leading us to the next new style, the transparent style, where the use of stems and lines are worked in an overlapping manner, creating a transparent volume mainly used as accents in plant arrangements. Florists have never been so well educated and equipped! With different styles, important theoretical knowledge of colours, shapes, rhythm, contrast and proportion, the challenge is to find an expression and a connection between fashion, interior and flowers. There is rapid development and an urge to find new flowers, varieties, foliage as well as accessories. This combined with working out the different styles, turned flower design into an inventive and trendy product bought by everyone.

Nowadays we see the importance of design and personal expression come before style. But still, plant arrangements as we present in this book are not as well appreciated and used as bouquets, as gifts, as well as for decorating our own homes. They don't always match the interior nor strengthen the interior's character. Looking back we see how flowers used to be an important part of an interior, completing it, not only adorning it by chance! It is time for a change and to make plant arrangement popular again.
The three of us are confident that with the knowledge, inspiration and a great selection of flowers, plants and accessories and materials at hand, all we need to do is to show the possibilities for using plant arrangements in interior design. Allowing historical influences to have an impact on design evolution and inspiring new designs and expressions, gives us the opportunity to create a new market that meets the unknown demands of the flower interested public!

Typical seventies style plant arrangement.

12

The future of the plant arrangement

In retrospect we think all florists can agree that plant arrangements have been left behind in the development of our profession and products. There is a huge potential with plants and plant arrangement, both from an environmental perspective as well as in terms of general lifestyle. Nowadays we spend more money and energy than ever on creating a comfortable home and a warm nest. Lets match this need of a conveniently designed home with fantastic plant arrangements!

Expression of emotions, personality and moods have become the driving force for today's florists, creating more individual, personalized and customized items. We are working towards a more personal touch, either reflecting the personality of the florist, the wishes of the customer or the uniqueness of the receiver. Doing this, we invent new designs and techniques, exciting shapes and refreshing colour combinations. The introduction of new materials brings a new dynamic into our profession. These botanical and artificial novelties are making it possible to translate individuality and emotions of people.

The way to decorate interiors has changed in the last years. Plants and plant arrangements will be chosen to match the room and are no longer foreign objects in a room. People will put more effort in choosing materials that reflect their own personality. Through our designs we can lead people into different moods. Even without flowers, the arrangements will be telling. We bring nature back into our interior, to enjoy its beauty and harmonizing power.

The success of do-it-yourself and total makeover programs on TV show that people are growing more aware of the interior surrounding them. Interior design has become one of people's main hobbies. A whole new generation of customers has stood up, waiting to be inspired and led by us, as florists! This gives us more possibilities than we can fathom. We just need to show what is possible and how plant arrangements, when integrated in a design or concept, can lift a whole room. We need to attract media attention and jump aboard this trend before it passes us by.

Arrangements can be a barometer of the times and are at the same time indicators for the qualities and market value of the designer. We already see customers looking for their 'own' designer and 'their' shop, reflecting 'their' tastes in design and style, 'their' situation and aesthetics. Knowledge of our product, special skills, and techniques to translate the wishes of the customer will become increasingly important to us.

Every customer is looking for a product fitting their unique taste and personal style. Everyone wants to find their unique plant arrangement!

Florists have to lead trends at all times; we should not be afraid to use new combinations of colours, materials and styles. Look at plants, both flowering and green ones and discover the differences in their personalities!

All the above is very important, to attract and to keep the new generation of buyers interested. Of course we must not forget the customers we already have. That is why we should remember our historical examples and the classic way of working.

Our skills and imagination combined with our ability to express emotions will be the key to success and will hopefully enable us to create long lasting impressions. Unique and long-living designs for individuals and interiors.

We hope that this book provides you with lots of inspiration and ideas, so that we, together, can build this market for the future.

Step by step

Springtime

Designer
Per
Materials
Betula / birch
Muscari / grape hyacinths
dry floral foam spheres
pheasant feathers
plant soil
spray paint (brown or black)
stub wire

1 Gather all materials and make sure to use *Muscari* that are already showing some colour, these are far more nice than green ones. Dry and stiff *Betula* twigs are no good in this arrangement, only freshly cut, flexible ones will do.

2 Carve out the upper third of the foam sphere to allow place for the bulbs. Spray paint the outside and the edges black, to make sure that no light coloured foam will shine through the *Betula* twigs.

3 Use the dry foam sphere and the stub wire to fasten the *Betula*. Push them into the ball at a low angle and secure them into place with U-shaped pieces of wire. Make sure to attach the *Betula* with the softer top parts towards the sun, so they fold out nicely.

4 When planting, try to make it look as if the *Muscari* are pushing through the *Betula* twigs. As if spring is forcing itself up through the barren branches.

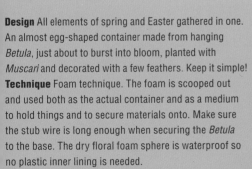

Design All elements of spring and Easter gathered in one. An almost egg-shaped container made from hanging *Betula*, just about to burst into bloom, planted with *Muscari* and decorated with a few feathers. Keep it simple!
Technique Foam technique. The foam is scooped out and used both as the actual container and as a medium to hold things and to secure materials onto. Make sure the stub wire is long enough when securing the *Betula* to the base. The dry floral foam sphere is waterproof so no plastic inner lining is needed.
Emotions There is hope for spring! See how life is fighting winter and is already sending the message of warmer sunnier days in early spring. Winter might still be reigning outside with snow and cold, but in the end spring will win. Simply give it a helping hand!

5 Accentuate the power of spring with more flexible *Betula* branches in between the *Muscari*. Make it look as if they forcefully had to make way for the coming of spring. As a final touch weave in some dark brown pheasant feathers to give the plant arrangement the feel of Easter.

Jungle of orchids

Designer
Tomas
Materials
Passiflora (passion flower)
Orchids (different types)
Slices of soft timber
Long, thin nails
Moss-covered branches
Clay

Design An exotic arrangement that takes its inspiration from the tropics. Epiphytes live on other plants, often trees, without being parasitic. The vertical arrangement refers to their natural habitat and way of growing: as epiphytes fight for light, they try to climb to the tops of the trees.

Technique A solid wooden base supports the vertical branches. These are nailed down vertically and form a support structure for the plants. This construction forms part of the concept. Epiphytes are not parasitic; they merely use it as a support. Real epiphytes rely on the atmosphere for their water and food supplies. This is why they should not be planted up in soil.

Emotions The jungle of orchids is exciting to behold. The freedom of the lines stands for our own free will and different personalities in society which form a harmonious entity. In other words: how balance can be brought about by random lines after all ...

1 Start with a square piece of wood (90cm by 90cm) with an opening (30cm by 30cm) in the centre. Cover with slices of birch (or other soft wood) of different sizes and nail down until the entire surface area is covered.

2 Use long nails to attach the moss-covered branches firmly to the base. Nail these down and cut off the heads, which makes it easier to attach the moss-covered branches. It is important to secure all the sticks since they will support all the plants. Avoid screws as these could split the branches.

3 Wash the orchids in a bucket with tepid water to remove any soil and wood chippings and to clean the aerial roots.

4 Finally, arrange the orchids evenly across the arrangement. Do not tie them too tightly to the branches. Distribute them making sure you create a certain sense of order in the plant chaos: the design and lines should remain visible. Quite a challenge!

Wild imagination

Designer
Max
Materials
Clematis
Gentiana
Iris germanica
Viola
Concrete container
Moss
Potting compost
Yoghurt

Design A plant arrangement specially designed for a small balcony. To create a natural effect, the concrete container is covered in yoghurt. When it goes green in time, it will blend in with the same rough and natural look of the plants.
Technique Interesting here is the use of yoghurt to change the look of materials. Make sure the plants are handled correctly and carefully before and during planting.
Emotion The arrangement has a very natural look, but the choice of blues and greys adds a cool, summery twist.

1 Cover the concrete pot with yoghurt, so that in time, it will be covered in moss and will blend in with the plants.

2 Give all the plants a good soak before arranging them.

3 Squeeze the flower pots to dislodge the plants from the pots to ensure the root system is not damaged.

4 When planting up, start on one side and work your way to the other side. Add more potting compost as and when needed from the side. This is easier and in that way, the soil can be pressed down easily as well. Plant up in small, natural groups, thus creating flowing lines. Add the *Clematis* tendrils at the very end to add even more movement. Cover up the soil with a layer of moss.

Entangled

Designer
Per
Materials
Dendrobium
Erica
cotton yarn
floral foam/Styrofoam sphere
stub wirers
orchid soil

1 Colour and general organic feel are the main features in this plant arrangement. Make sure that the colours of the *Dendrobium*, the *Erica* and all types and thicknesses of yarn correspond harmonically.

2 Start by creating the container for the plant arrangement. Carve out the inside of a dry floral foam sphere. When prefered, a styrofoam sphere can be used. Both materials are waterproof so no plastic inner lining is necessary.

3 To decorate the outside of the sphere, work *Erica* and yarn in a mixed overlapping manner. Cut a sharp point to the *Erica* stalks, insert them lengthwise in the foam and secure them in place with yarn. Continue until the entire foam surface is covered.

4 Plant the *Dendrobiums* in the sphere using special orchid soil that keeps the rootsystem moist and airy. Observe the direction of flowers and foliage to create a general flow.

5 Once planted, continue to decorate over the orchid base. To integrate the ball shape and the *Dendrobium*, use pieces of yarn reinforced with iron thread. In this way it is possible to curve the yarn over the orchid soil and to continue the spherical shape throughout.

Design A decorative, spherical plant arrangement focusing on colours and a general organic feel. For the container we use one type of plant, the *Erica*, and yarn to accentuate with the deep purple *Dendrobium*. The colour of the *Dendrobium* is emphasized with purples, lilacs, browns and pinks.
Technique Basic plant technique using orchid soil to keep the orchid roots moist and airy. Foam is used, both as a container and as a medium to fix the *Erica* onto.
Emotions Deep dark colours create a more mysterious autumn feel than the more obvious orange tones. Mixing an exotic material like *Dendrobium* with the more rustic *Erica* gives a feel of the modern mixed world we are living in today.

23

Triptych of Muscari

Designer
Tomas
Materials
Slate
Muscari (grape hyacinth)
Magic gel crystal soil
Hot glue gun

Design The impact of a triptych in combination with the force of nature makes for a particularly strong design. The daintiness and fragility of the *Muscari* in flower is in stark contrast with the roughness of the slate. The design is clean and simple so that all eyes can be fixed on that one flowering plant: the *Muscari*.
Technique Placing the slate is the most labour-intensive part of this arrangement. The slate is inserted in the floral foam and glued in place. Plant up the *Muscari* in the remaining area of the dish.
Emotions The force of spring that makes these flowers come into flower is magical. Growing, flowering and the will and power to develop are all elements that typify human life too.

Triptych of Muscari

1 To create flowing lines across the dishes, place them in a row and mark the desired line with a pen. This will ensure that the lines continue across the three dishes. Next, cut the floral foam according to the lines and scoop out the centre.

2 Placing the slate takes up most time in this plant arrangement. Press the slate down firmly in the floral foam and create different layers, both heightwise and lengthwise. In that way, we obtain a natural line and a rough structure. Glue the slate in place here and there.

3 Next, plant up the *Muscari* in the space provided. Make sure the bulbs are clearly visible in this arrangement.

4 To finish off, sprinkle blue and transparent magic gel crystal soil over the arrangement. The blue colour echoes the colour of the *Muscari* in flower. Thanks to the harmony in colour, both plant and dish blend in perfectly.

5 Place the dishes next to each other as a triptych. Optically, this creates the illusion that the lines of the slate and flowers blend.

Happy christmas

Designer
Max

Materials
Cetraria islandica (Iceland moss)
Phalaenopsis (two plants)
Mossy branches
Glue gun
Plastic Christmas baubles
Cold glue

1 Use sharp scissors to cut off the tops of the baubles. Glue them into a dish shape with the glue gun. Reinforce them by gluing them together in different places. Use a flat dish as a mould. This will make it easier to work and create an even shape.

2 Use the cold glue to fill the gaps between the baubles with the coloured Iceland moss. Spread the colours evenly. Glue a gnarled, mossy branch in and across the dish.

3 Remove the *Phalaenopsis* from the pot and carefully clean the aerial roots. Needless to say, these plants need a good watering before planting.

4 Carefully but firmly tie the *Phalaenopsis* onto the moss-covered branch, preferably off-centre, to add interest. Water the roots daily for maximum longevity.

Design An unexpected combination, a strong shape that is attractive thanks to its sense of calm and simplicity. The choice of materials sets the tone: a Christmas atmosphere, yet subdued and modestly elegant.
Technique The glue gun is most effective, but if you make it with cold glue, the dish will be stronger and more water resistant. Using a mould makes it easier to get the shape right. An uneven edge adds interest.
Emotion The sparkly baubles lend the piece instant Christmas interest. The gold colour adds warmth to the design. Contained within the festive dish, there appears to exist another, calmer world.

29

Black velvet

Designer
Per
Materials
Begonia
Senecio Senetti(R) 'Deep Blue'
Christmas baubles
feathers
hot glue gun
plant soil
black French vase
wooden skewers

Design The high gloss black baroque French vase has a traditional shape, but its shiny black surface hints at modern times. The flowers and materials are rather traditional too and fit into the same époque. The total absence of green creates an almost non-botanical/artificial expression.

Technique Ordinary planting technique. The decorative elements are added by wiring and gluing. The treatment of the *Senecio* is a bit harsh, but it is all for the sake of the expression in the final arrangement. The plant is not damaged, simply pruned.

Emotions Dark, mysterious, consuming, rich in expression and with a very unexpected colour scheme to get that special *wow factor*. This is how we can make plant arrangements popular again. Show what can be done, entertain and enthral people!

1 Choose materials with a baroque feel to them, ranging from blue to black, shiny to math, high gloss to velvet and from smooth to rough textures.

2 Glue the Christmas baubles onto wooden skewers and cut these to the same length as the plant materials. Attach some feathers to stub wire to secure them in place in a later stadium.

3 Plant the *Begonia* and *Senecio* in a mixed pattern. Try to clear as much of its green foliage as possible and arrange the *Senecio* in between the black *Begonia* leaves as to minimize the amount of green as much as possible.

4 Work as mixed as possible as far as the decorative part is concerned. The single and main focus should be to cover all green leaves to get an almost non-botanical, but very dramatic blue/black expression.

5 Work in all materials in a mixed way, to create contrast and positive tension in between the materials. Think in contrasts: black versus blue, matt versus high gloss, and small versus big.

31

Sense of security

Designer
Tomas
Materials
Poinsettia (Christmas flower)
Decorative container
Christmas baubles
Small waterproof container
Felt wire (two different colours)
Potting compost
Felt fabric

Design Felt is a user-friendly material that is becoming increasingly popular. Felting is not new, but the materials are currently available in many different, fresh colours, so that the prettiest combinations can be created. We have kept things simple and warm in this arrangement, in keeping with the cosy Christmas period.
Technique Felting as a technique to make materials without weaving them has been around for ages. Felt is snug and warm and attractive to boot. A user-friendly material with many options for the florist thanks to the many colours and processing methods. Since felt is not waterproof, use an extra vase for the plants in the arrangement.
Emotion The need to snuggle up, literally and figuratively speaking, goes hand in hand with Christmas. Centrally placed *Poinsettias*, wrapped in warm felt, evoke a snug and safe feeling that typifies that time of year.

1 We have opted for a colour scheme ranging from golden yellow to beige, brown and gold to dark brown. The felt thread reflects these colours, which results in harmony. The Christmas baubles add difference in texture and form, and add volume to the creation.

2 Place a smaller, waterproof receptacle in the main dish. To create tension, place it off-centre. Next use the felt. Wrap it around the small container and extend into the space between the two receptacles until this area is completely covered.

3 Fill the central, waterproof pot with *Poinsettias*. Plant these just below the pot's edge so that the felt or the wooden container do not get wet when watering.

4 Guide the felt thread through and over the felt. An orderly set of lines adds movement and extra emotion to the arrangement.

5 Use Christmas baubles to finish off the design. Start with the larger ones and continue with the smaller ones. Add sophistication by adding a few smaller, richly decorated baubles.

33

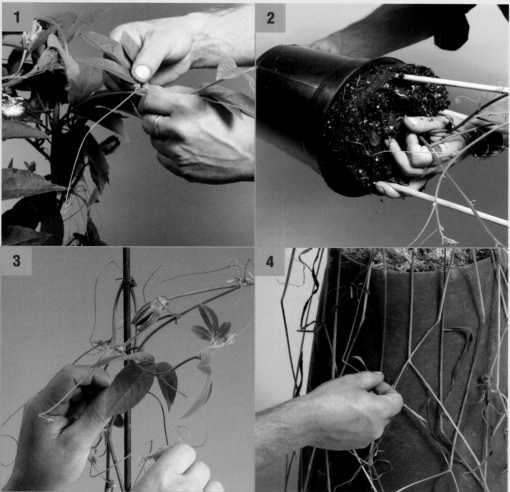

Disected in beauty

Designer
Max
Materials
Passiflora / passion flower
Flowering grasses (of your choice)
Potting compost
2 metal rods (2m long and 8mm wide)
Cold glue

Design By removing the leaves, the natural lines of
the *Passiflora* are enhanced. The grasses lend the
arrangement a natural and transparent look.
By accentuating the shape of the pot with grasses,
the plant arrangement becomes a work of art, with the
container forming an organic part of it.
Technique Removing the leaves makes the plant less
sensitive to drought and encourages tendril growth. It is
also important to give the plants a good soak and make
sure the root system is not damaged whilst re-potting.
Emotions A contemporary plant arrangement for the
patio with an airy, frivolous look. Since the growth
and flowering pattern of the *Passiflora* changes daily,
the arrangement continues to excite until the winter.

1 Take the *Passiflora* apart, remove ¾ of the leaves,
but retain the buds.

2 Submerge the plants in water until they are saturated.
By squeezing the side of the pot, the plant comes out
easily without damaging the roots.

3 Fill the pot with potting compost and plant the
Passiflora. Plant up to 10cm under the rim of the pot.
Insert the metal rods into the soil and loosely wind
the *Passiflora* tendrils around the rods.

4 Attach the long grasses to the outside of the pot with
cold glue. Plait them upwards to combine with the
Passiflora. Respect the shape of the pot when plaiting.
The higher the pot, the fewer the grasses. Leave 1/3 of
the top of the *Passiflora* grass-free, to give the *Passiflora*
all the attention it deserves.

Spring romance

Designer
Tomas
Materials
Adiantum raddianum (Maidenhair fern)
Hydrangea
Jasminum (jasmine)
Aluminium wire
Clay pellets
Decorative ribbons (different types)
Styrofoam hemisphere
Potting soil

Design Use a big plant pot that is not too heavy on the eye. Thanks to a combination of light and transparent Maidenhair fern on the one hand and robust *Hydrangea* on the other, we can strike the right balance.
The jasmine tendrils add a sense of airiness to the arrangement. The richly adorned rim adds harmony between the colours and creates unity.
Technique The main technique is this arrangement is wrapping the styrofoam with multi-coloured ribbons of different textures and thicknesses. Jasmine tendrils add a playful touch. This is why it is important to drape them over the entire arrangement.
Emotions A romantic spring feeling thanks to the colours and choice of plants. Once again, we manage to evoke emotions with our creations and actions. Let the colours and plants do the talking.

1 The main ingredient of this plant arrangement is the styrofoam hemisphere. Choose ribbons, a dish and plants in one and the same colour scheme. Choose one type of ribbon in a contrasting colour. Clay pellets and potting compost are also essential.

2 Cut the bottom of the styrofoam so that it fits snugly in the dish. Wrap ribbons around the styrofoam and finish off with the ribbon in the contrasting colour. Aluminium colours add a distinct sense of opulence.

3 Fill the bottom with clay pellets and plant the jasmine in the centre of the dish. Plant it quite deep so that small *Hydrangea* plants can be added on top. Distribute the jasmine branches evenly across the entire dish.

4 Plant the *Hydrangea* and Adiantum at random but make sure they are evenly distributed. Let the *Adiantum* leaves trail loosely through and over the *Hydrangea* so that the two plants can merge in natural harmony.

5 To make the vase and plant blend in, drape the jasmine tendrils across both. It connects both receptacles and adds a sense of airiness to the arrangement.

37

Autumns gold

Designer
Per
Materials
Acer (leaves)
Cymbidium
Fittonia
Malus
Nertera
fibreglass container
pearl headed needles
plant soil
plastic water tubes
spray glue
stub wire

Design A round, domed almost traditional plant arrangement where the decorative accents are the most important feature. Use one type of plant to create a calm backdrop, and work at one single height. Go for similarities instead of contrasts. Add tension and contrast with well chosen accents.

Technique Ordinary planting technique. When needed, secure the *Nertera* with stub wire because they usually have a badly developed root system. Pinning and piercing techniques for the decorative accents. Take care not to damage any of the plants when pinning them on. Work in between and not on top of the other materials.

Emotions Autumn at its best. Nature is dressed in warm yellows and oranges, even the browns look amazing when caressed by the warmth of the sun. Autumn is not the season for depression, it is a time for joy and happiness.

Autumns gold

1 Start with a morning walk in the autumn sun and collect the most stunning *Acer* leaves for your plant arrangement. Get the feel and scents of nature when the sun warms it up. Let the leaves dry thoroughly before working with them.

2 Use any odd, left over container, clean it and start by covering its surface with the dry *Acer* leaves. Place 10-15 leaves on paper, lightly spray them with glue and let them rest for at least a minute before applying them to the container. This way they will stick a lot better. Overlap the leaves at least 1cm to allow shrinkage.

3 Once the outside surface and the visible part of the inside of the container is covered in leaves, start planting the *Nertera*. Plant them in any desired pattern, but in big clean groups. All of the decorative accents will be added later on, so it is important to keep the background calm and subtle.

4 Prepare all extra materials: add pins to the leaves, stub wire to the apples and put the orchid flowers in plastic tubes. These tubes provide the flowers with enough water to last at least a week. Decorate the surface to enhance the colours and to give the arrangement an extraordinary expression.

Family do

Designer
Max
Materials
Paphiopedilum
Moss
Brown aluminium wire
Brown binding wire
Styrofoam hemispheres (with a 30cm diameter)
Copper-coloured stars
Potting compost
Spray glue
White wax
White paper

1 Glue the two hemispheres together and cut out a wedge. Flatten the bottom of the sphere so that it can sit up. Attach white paper to the sphere by means of spray glue. This provides a better base for the wax.

2 Heat up the wax on the hob. Do not overheat the wax to avoid it becoming too transparent or too runny. Cover the entire sphere with wax for a good adhesive layer. Create a decorative drip effect with a spoon.

3 Attach the stars to the aluminium wire with binding wire. Make sure the orchids had a good watering before use.

4 Fill the spheres with a layer of orchid potting compost and plant the *Paphiopedilum* in the spheres. Cover up with moss. Make sure you plant the plants sufficiently deep. This makes it easier to water them. The wedge is accentuated by decorative stars on aluminium wire.

Design A design with traditional Christmas materials and shapes. Using the materials in an unusual way adds a modern twist. A festive decoration which, thanks to its simplicity, would suit many interiors.
Technique Make sure you use a layer of paper between the styrofoam and the wax. The temperature determines the thickness of the wax and is important for a perfect result. Make sure the bottom of the sphere remains closed.
Emotion The spheres presented in a group evoke a family. Self-willed creations, personal, retiring and exuding warmth. Much like a cosy family get-together.

43

Frostbitten

Designer
Per
Materials
Erica
Juniperus
Picea
plant soil
round container
aluminium wire
metal angelhair
bullion wire

Design A plant arrangement for outdoor use. Therefore it is important to thoroughly think through the choice of colours and decorative elements. It is very important to use and to perfect our floristic skills for outdoor plant arrangements.

Technique Plant technique with sturdy and long lasting plants that can conquer the cold winter days. It is very important to find decorative techniques that last just as long and stay beautiful throughout the lifespan of the plants. Secure the materials in place, so all will survive unpredictable weather!

Emotions Longing for snow, frost and cold days. But with the weather getting unpredictable, we dont know if snow is coming or not. So why not create that winter feeling with plants and well chosen accesories.

1 In this outdoor plant arrangement I chose materials that in colour and texture have a frosted greyish feel and look.This to give the arrangement a wintery feel of snow and frost. All materials are tones of grey, spanning from green to turquoise and silver grey.

2 When planting, create a very clean and simple grouping. Make one circular shape and a moon crest. Make sure to keep each colour within the boundaries of its shape, but do not hesitate to mix plants within each segment. For example *Juniperus* and *Picea* can be mixed, for they are in the same colour tone. *Picea* branches are not planted, only inserted into the soil.

3 Create decorative spirals from aluminium wire and attach them to a sprig of *Picea* with metal angelhair and bullion wire. This makes them both prettier and more easy to secure them in the plant arrangement. Mix colours but pick one dominant colour.

4 Place the different sized spirals into the plant arrangement in a playful overlapping pattern. They are the link between the two main shapes in the design. We now have one bigger spiral shape formed by the plants, with a top layer of smaller decorative spirals, creating a dynamic expression.

Twins

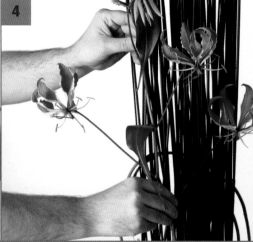

Designer
Tomas
Materials
Fargesia (black)
Gloriosa superba 'Rothschildiana' (glory lily)
Clay pellets
Wire and ribbons
Potting compost
Floral foam
Two black, oriental vases

Design The combination of the exotic *Gloriosa* with the two black vases give the plant arrangement a mystical, oriental look. The plants can easily grow as tall as 2 metres, a characteristic that is accentuated in this clean, vertical design. The flowers are quite dominant and like quite a bit of freedom of movement. It is a game of give and take, where the character of the plants is respected.
Technique Before planting up *Gloriosa*, place a block of floral foam at the bottom of the vase in which the *Fargesia* can be inserted at a later stage. Place these carefully to create a parallel arrangement, giving the *Gloriosa* the necessary support while avoiding an untidy finish.
Emotions The flowers flutter like butterflies through the arrangement. Enjoy their beauty, their colour and simple elegance. The flowers form the melody of the arrangement, much like we are the melody of our lives.

1 In addition to the striking *Gloriosa* we use floral foam and a few *Fargesia* sticks. Aluminium wire and leather straps finish off the arrangement.

2 Place the floral foam at the bottom of the vase. Make sure it covers the entire base of the vase and is firmly in place. Fill the base with clay pellets, plant up *Gloriosa* and press down firmly.

3 In order to add interest to the black bamboo sticks, wrap some wire around them at irregular intervals. The texture and colour of the wire are important. Red emphasizes the flowers, while black adds sophistication. The leather strap adds softness to the otherwise rigid, crimson piece.

4 When inserting the *Fargesia*, make sure they are pressed down into the floral foam. Work with care and make sure that all the sticks stand up straight to create an attractive and orderly entity.
Finally, weave the plant through the construction.
To create an attractive and orderly entity, remove any leaves that are too big.

47

Over-flowing

Designer
Max
Materials
Sedum
Potting compost
2 dishes
Metal pokers (1mm diameter)
Cold glue

1 Fill the first dish from the centre with potting compost. Make sure the soil is not too dry, otherwise it will be difficult to plant up.

2 The *Sedum* is planted up from the sides, closely together, and firmly pressed down with potting compost and secured with a poker or attached to each other.

3 Fill up the entire outside and inside ring, whilst trying to achieve a straight, even edge. Potting compost is added on top of the arrangement which is covered with the second dish.

4 Attach loose *Sedum* plants with cold glue on the top dish, starting from the centre and working your way to the edge. Water regularly so that the plants can continue growing.

Design The arrangement is a testament to nature's force of survival. The plants start in the middle and grow in every direction in a slow, natural movement.
Technique The choice of material is the single most important factor in this design. Succulents can survive on very little indeed, which means they can be used in arrangements where other plants would wither and die. Always consider the chances of survival of the plants when planning arrangements.
Emotion A creation filled with hope. However badly we treat nature and the planet, there will always be plant and animal species which, in time, restore the balance and repair what we have destroyed.

49

Striped

Designer
Per

Materials
Sanseveria rotundifolia / mother-in-law's tongue
bullion wire
Mizuhiki wire
pheasant feathers
plant soil
porcupine quills
small white pebbles
square wooden container

Design Stripes in varying colours, sizes and textures.
A contemporary translation of art deco and its contrasting
colours, dark and light, metallic and math, soft and hard.
Plants go fashion! Make your own Coco Chanel or Jean
Paul Gaultier.
Technique Normal planting techniques, wiring for the
feathers and piercing for the quills and wired feathers.
Piercing the leaves with thin wire and sharp quills does
not cause any long term damage to the plant.
Emotions Sharp, clean and modern. An excellent look for
contemporary spaces with a lot of glass, steel and stone.
A look adapted to the 21st century instead of the lush
generous expression we are used to. One has to show
both ends of the spectrum, demonstrate all possibilities
with plants, to reach all possible plant lovers.

1 Think of contrasts when gathering materials for this
plant arrangement, but within a well-defined theme to
keep things simple and coherent. Stripes in contrasting
colours, lighter and darker ones.

2 Prepare all feathers by wiring them onto Mizuhiki wire
using black bullion wire. Clean the porcupine quills to
avoid damaging the plants when piercing the leaves.

3 Plant the *Sanseverias* deep enough to allow adding
a rich layer of clear white pebbles. This as a great
contrast between the square container and the
grey-green *Sanseveria*.

4 For the decoration: first work in the wired feathers and
make sure they are put in at about the same angle, but in
opposite direction as the lines of the *Sanseveria* leaves.
Make the feathers end at about the same height too.
The porcupine quills are then inserted at a sharper angle
more matching the wallpaper in the background. These
will also lock and keep the Mizuhiki wire in position.

51

Natural force

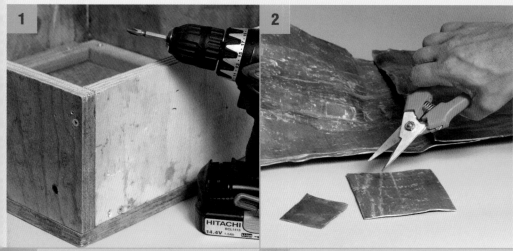

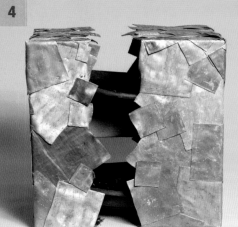

Designer
Max

Materials
Lewisia cotyledon
Passiflora
Sedum
Wood (waterproof plywood)
Sheet of lead
Plastic saucers
Nails

1 Make two open crates from waterproof plywood with a surface area of 50cm. The first crate should be 20cm high, the second 15cm. The two are attached with a bottom and middle layer, creating an open cube. Place plastic saucers for the plants on the bottom and middle layers.

2 Cut squares of different sizes from the lead. Use thin lead, which weighs less and is easier to manipulate. Preferably use a sheet of old and new lead, which makes for exciting colour shades, or treat the lead with hydrochloric acid to obtain a similar effect.

3 The lead is attached to the cube with nails. Create a random arrangement of squares, avoiding parallels and horizontal or vertical lines.

4 Make sure the plants have had a good soak before planting. Remove ¼ of the leaves of the *Passiflora* before planting up. The *Passiflora* adds movement, while the *Sedum* creates depth. All plants must be firmly firmed up in the soil for improved rooting.

Design The lead cube looks indestructible, yet the fragile, brightly-coloured flowers easily rip open the robust cube, which suggest immense natural power. A design that plays with contrasting materials and colours.
Technique Use a good-quality wood to make sure the object will last. Make sure you use plants that can be kept a long time and treat the materials respectfully and carefully when planting them up.
Emotions Working with contrast and playing with the forces of nature can result in special creations of which you will never tire. To make a design exciting and intriguing, it is important to suggest maximum movement.

54

Eternal love

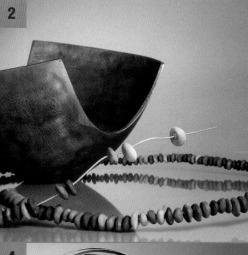

Designer
Tomas
Materials
Calamus rotang (rattan)
Clematis
Moss
Raku pebbles
Strong wire

1 An elegant U-shaped vase is combined with wire circles. Raku pebbles and grey-purple rattan blend in with the purple *Clematis*. Moss adds the finishing touch.

2 Thread the Raku pebbles on a piece of strong wire. Alternate black and white pebbles to create a lovely colour effect.

3 This step is the most challenging one. Bend the wire into a circle and try to do this as smoothly as possible. Do the same with the flexible rattan and attach to the Raku circles.

4 Firmly press down the soil in the dish so that the circles remain in place. Do not start planting up the *Clematis* until then. Plant up in such a way as to ensure that the lines of the tendrils mimic the circular movement.

5 Plant up the moss before attaching the tendrils to the rattan and Raku circles as this reduces the risk of breaking any tendrils.

Design Now and then, we commemorate our loved ones who have passed away with a bunch of flowers or a plant. A design that is serene thanks to the colour and yet stylish thanks to the choice of plants and materials used. A creation which allows us to demonstrate our affection and bond with a close friend or relative who has died.
Technique No climbing plant flowers as profusely as the *Clematis*. This climber thrives in full sunlight or against a warm wall or fence. A rattan and Raku pebble construction supports the *Clematis*. Moss is both decorative and functional as it prevents the plant from drying out.
Emotions The circle of life, combined with the splendour of *Clematis*. We are grateful for the love we received from our loved ones and treasure the precious moments and warm memories.

Watch out, it's an illusion!

Designer
Per
Materials
cactuses
cardboard
container
fake fur
pearl-headed pins
cactus soil
plastic ribbons
spray glue
stub wire
wool yarn

Design Who really likes cactuses besides kids? These little things are bought once, but are not very attractive and thus easily forgotten. Making something spectacular out of something very ordinary is a true art. This arrangement plays with the illusion of softness, inside one of my favourite shapes; the dome. There is no better shape to display materials and to work with decorative accents.
Technique Plant technique, use special cactus soil and gloves when planting. This is better for the plant and for you. Wiring, spinning and pinning are done with respect for the plants. Do not pierce the cactus, it would kill the plant.
Emotions Soft, relaxing and inviting. Who does not want to rest their head on this soft cushion? The illusion is perfect, nothing is what it seems to be.

1 In this arrangement we use the often misunderstood cactus. We contrast the prickly plant with the fake fur to create an illusion of softness. Which material is soft and which one is not?

2 Start by creating a circular, slightly domed structure out of cardboard reinforced with stub wire in between the two layers of paper. Use ordinary tape for doing this. Attach the fake fur using spray glue.

3 Wrap wool around wooden skewers or stub wire. Make sure to make these spools thicker in the centre.

4 Use special soil for cactuses, which has more sand and allows better drainage. For your own health and happiness, use gloves when planting.

57

Watch out, it's an illusion!

5

5 Trim and fluff the fake fur so it connects better with the cactuses. Place the yarn covered skewers on top of the arrangement, but do so in an overlapping manner to connect the cactuses and fur and to smoothen out the domed shape.

6 Finally attach lines of black, liquorice-like plastic ribbon, repeating the overlapping pattern of the yarn covered skewers. Secure all accents with black pearl-headed pins.

6

Azalea with a twist

Designer
Tomas
Materials
Rhododendron simssii (indoor azalea)
Corypha (dried) (Gebang Palm)
Clay pellets
Bamboo sticks
Decorative snow
Potting compost

Design The azalea, the showpiece of Belgium's ornamental plant cultivation, sometimes suffers from an old-fashioned image. Nevertheless, it offers many creative possibilities and certainly fits into any trendy front room. Create a contemporary look where the plant and receptacle blend into one. A lidded dish gives the plant a totally different look.

Technique Create a lively arrangement by planting up the azalea at an angle, facing outwards. Bamboo sticks hold the lid in place so that it does not damage the plants. Twigs of dried *Corypha* are woven through the plants.

Emotion Create a wintery effect by using white azaleas and decorative snow. The beauty, personality and flowering method of the azalea play the lead role. The azalea has plenty of character.

1 For effective drainage, fill the bottom of the vase with clay pellets. Before planting up, give the azaleas a good soak in a bucket of water and remove any flowers that have left off so that new buds can emerge. Plant up all around the sides, but leave the centre free.

2 To make sure the lid does not squash the plants, make a sturdy construction using bamboo sticks. Make sure they are level and spread the sticks evenly so that the lid is stable.

3 Place the lid level. Finish off with dried *Corypha* twigs around the lid and the vase. To enhance the harmony of colour and evoke a wintery atmosphere, paint the twigs white.

4 Wrap the twigs between the plants and on top of the vase. Now and then, place the twigs above the flowers to add extra movement. Spray ornamental snow here and there to add an extra wintery accent.

61

In his element

Designer
Max
Materials
Sarracenia
Sphagnum (peat moss)
Container (waterproof)
Clay granules

1 To establish proper water drainage, fill one third of the container with clay granules. Cover with a layer of *Sphagnum*, which will retain the water and has a high acidity level, which is ideal for *Sarracenias*.

2 Fill the container with *Sphagnum* up to 10cm below the edge. Give the plants a good soaking before use. Remove them from their pots carefully, trying not to damage the roots.

3 Plant up the *Sarracenia* in the *Sphagnum*. Make sure the roots are in good contact with the moss. Plant up the plants in groups, as they would grow naturally. Do make sure the end result is in harmony. Place fresh pieces of wood covered in moss in between the plants. Do this randomly to achieve a natural look.

4 This plant composition, which can be displayed inside or outside, should be kept moist. Since bog plants are used that must not dry out, it is important to water them regularly. The moss on the wood is a good gauge for the moisture level of the arrangement as a whole. If you work with fresh *Sphagnum*, you will notice that after a period of drought, it will, if given proper care, recover.

Design A container with one plant species. Plant the plants deeper than usual to obtain an interesting balance and to add an element of surprise. The wood covered in fresh moss, in combination with *Sphagnum*, makes it all very natural and is a lovely finishing touch.
Technique By starting off with a layer of clay pellets, we can reduce the risk of the plant roots being constantly wet. The *Sphagnum* adds the finishing touch but, above all, guarantees the correct acidity and water levels. Make sure all the roots make firm contact with the *Sphagnum*.
Emotion The power of simplicity, robust and wild, yet contained. Strong colours exuding calmness, a little world within our world, a patch of nature in our environment.

Budding spring

Designer
Tomas
Materials
Betula (bark)
Narcissus
Clay pellets
Moss
Potting compost
Ornamental diamonds
Spray snow
Hot glue

Design Budding daffodils stand for spring. The feeling of spring is played out to the full in this design as you can see the plants open up one by one: a true spectacle of nature. An arrangement that brings spring into your home, holding, as it does, the promise of sun and warmth.
Technique Break off the bark of birch into strips and attach to the vase, merely for decorative purposes. Plant up the daffodils just as they are producing green shoots so that they can develop from bulb to mature flower. Spray snow and glistening diamonds give the arrangement a wintery look.
Emotions We give the bulbs the freedom to develop. he possibility to let nature do what it has to do is one of the many joys of plant arrangements.

Budding spring

1 Rip large sheets of the bark of birch into strips. Make sure the strips are flexible and curved. This makes for a more fluid and more feminine result.

2 Use a glue gun to attach the strips of bark to the vase, to both the inside and the outside. Since warm glue does not stick well to aluminium, glue the tops of the inner and outer strips together to create a solid rim.

3 Before planting up the bulbs, start with a layer of clay pellets. They guarantee effective drainage and prevent the bulbs from rotting. Add a layer of potting compost and press the bulbs down firmly.

4 To finish off, fill the gaps with moss, but do not cover the bulbs, as these will put us in a spring mood. Fake snow reinforces the idea of changing from winter to early spring and a few ornamental diamonds create a wintery and sophisticated feeling.

Orchid balls

Designer
Per

Materials
Cattleya / Cattleya orchid
bullion wire
dry or fresh floral foam spheres
glue
metal skewers
moss
wool yarn

Design Create a natural habitat for the plants, but update it and make it more creative. An expression for a modern, ecology conscious plant lover. Playing with simple geometric shapes, allowing design and function to be joint.

Technique Binding techniques, both for the plants and for the decorative part of this arrangement. Moss and floral foam spheres are used as basis. Changing soil to moss for the *Cattleya* will resemble their natural habitat and improve their living conditions. Take good care of *Cattleya* orchids, closely follow the instructions on how and on how frequent to spray them.

Emotions Playful and young, almost childish. Come on and start juggling with these flower spheres. Do not always walk the well paved way of pots and containers, be daring!

1 Take your time to choose a colour spectrum. This arrangement is all about copper: so pick different shades of orange, brown and mustard. Look for rougher textures to correspond with the moss.

2 Create lots of different sized balls covered in yarn in a variety of colours, textures and thicknesses. Wrap the wool around fresh or dry floral foam or Styrofoam balls; any material will work as long as it can be pierced onto the metal stands. Finish the balls off with bullion wire in matching colours to secure the yarn and to add a shiny touch.

3 Bring the orchid back to its original way of growing, out of the soil and into the air. Create spheres of moss around the roots, to allow air and moisture to reach the orchid roots, but at the same time make the moss ball rather compact for stability. Secure the moss with bullion wire.

4 Arrange the different spheres in a playful and dynamic mix. Keep in mind the natural curves of the *Cattleya* and work accordingly. If needed, secure the bottom ball with glue so the stacked balls won't slide down the metal stand.

69

Force of spring

Designer
Max

Materials
Betula
Convallaria majalis
Galanthus nivalis
Jasminum polyanthum
Muscari
Narcissus 'Paper White'
Wire (1mm)
Glue gun
Flattened moss
Flat saucer (minimum diameter 30cm)
Potting compost

Design The plant dish exudes a powerful force; the fragile spring flowers rip the firm bark apart. The suggestion of movement adds interest to the arrangement. The choice of colours makes everything appear pure. The arrangement that blends in seamlessly with the table enhances this feeling.
Technique Carefully follow the steps. Make sure there is firm contact between the soil and the plants, and ensure that the soil in the centre is higher than at the edge. Plant up in a semi-circle and cover with moss.
Emotion A new start. Pure, shameless force, with new values and fresh energy. An ever recurrent cycle of switching generations.

Force of spring

1 Use secateurs to cut squares of different sizes (between 3 and 8cm) from the bark of *Betula*. Also cut a few pieces of wire to size (15cm) and loop one end with a pen. Bend these loops at 90-degree angles. Make thirty or so such wires, on which a square of bark is glued with the glue pistol. These will be used later to finish off the arrangement.

2 Fill the dish with potting compost. Make a mound in the middle and reduce the amount of soil towards the edge. Glue the largest squares of bark to the edge of the dish. Glue the other pieces randomly on top of these, thus creating a firm edge that rests on the table.

3 Give the plants a good soak before use. Remove most of the leaves of the *Jasminum* and break up the clumps of the other plants. Starting from the edge, plant up the dish completely. Then cover the soil with flattened moss. Leave some room between the plants so that bark can be added.

4 By inserting the bark on wire in between the plants, the spherical shape of the arrangement is enhanced. In between the spiked squares, smaller pieces of bark are glued. In that way, all the pieces of bark are connected. Make sure there is a space between the soil and the bark, which adds depth and volume to the arrangement.

Radius of slate

Designer
Tomas
Materials
Jovibarba sobolifera (houseleek)
Sedum spurium (rockcress)
Sempervivum arachnoideum (cobweb houseleek)
Sempervivum arachnoideum var. tomentosum
Sempervivum 'Commander Hay'
Sempervivum 'Rubin'
Potting compost
Clay pellets
Slate
Hot glue gun and glue cartridges
Silicone adhesive (for concrete and stone applications)

1 Look for a suitable vase with a wide horizontal rim on which the irregular pieces of slate can be attached. Use a hammer to break the slate into the desired size. Different types of *Sempervivum* make for a more interesting texture. Sort the different *Sempervivum* according to colour.

2 Use two different types of glue in this construction so that the arrangement is suitable for display both inside and outside. Silicone retains its adhesive powers in all weather conditions, while hot glue bonds instantly. Start off with a layer of silicone to attach the slate to the dish.

3 Next use the hot glue gun. When planting up, start in the centre and work your way outward. Start with the darkest *Sempervivum*.

4 Tear strips from larger plants and use these to plug any gaps in the design. Finally, brush off any excess soil/dirt to end up with a fine result.

Design Rays of slate, supplemented with plants that find their own way and continue growing. It is the lines in this design that steal the show. The simple colour and the plants create natural, simple beauty.
Technique Glue the slate to the dish. Use two types of glue. Start with the weatherproof silicone and then use the glue gun which glues the slate in place in an instant. The slate is placed from a central point and fans out like rays.
Emotion A design marked by coherence, but with attention to the individuality of the component parts. The closer to the centre, the stronger the bond between the plants. Unity breeds power. The awareness not to be alone in the universe gives a special feeling.

Soft and tender

Designer
Per
Materials
Campanula / bellflower
cardboard
glass container
plant soil
stub wire
tape
wool yarn

1 Trim and water the plants so they look really fresh. Whatever kind of plants you might want to use, search for plants in the same size and with the same height to create a clear, strong shape.

2 Make yarn covered neck rings for the glass containers. Start by cutting cardboard in the desired length and height and reinforce this cardboard strip by taping stub wire onto the paper.

3 The cardboard ring is covered in yarn. Work the wool in a mixed pattern, starting with the thickest and filling in the gaps with thinner wool. Make one ring for each container and some smaller, decorative ones for use in between the plants.

4 Place the fully planted glass container inside the yarn covered rings. Make sure that the plants you use are slightly overflowing the edges of the container to make a connection with the wool ring.

5 As a final touch we position the smaller rings in between the flowers to connect the base to the plant part. Using stub wire, these smaller rings are secured into the soil.

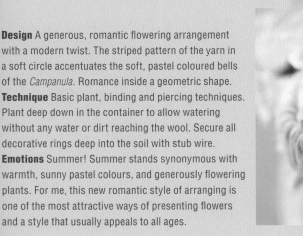

Design A generous, romantic flowering arrangement with a modern twist. The striped pattern of the yarn in a soft circle accentuates the soft, pastel coloured bells of the *Campanula*. Romance inside a geometric shape.
Technique Basic plant, binding and piercing techniques. Plant deep down in the container to allow watering without any water or dirt reaching the wool. Secure all decorative rings deep into the soil with stub wire.
Emotions Summer! Summer stands synonymous with warmth, sunny pastel colours, and generously flowering plants. For me, this new romantic style of arranging is one of the most attractive ways of presenting flowers and a style that usually appeals to all ages.

77

Natural feelings

1

2

Designer
Max
Materials
Equisetum / Horsetail
Sphagnum (peat moss)
Orchids (of your choice)
Cement
Potting compost
Water

3

4

Design This plant dish is made from natural-looking materials, which means the dish and arrangement can become one. The dish will become more attractive and more interesting with age. Keep it moist as we are using plants from a peat environment.

Technique It is important to prepare the dish well. If at all possible, mix up the turf with old plant roots for an attractive and strong finish. Make sure the cement is not spread out too thinly and give the dish enough time to dry.

Emotions A surprising plant dish for the garden, with a special, natural look. It seems as if the dish has simply been extracted from nature. This makes for harmony and relaxation in the garden and mind.

1 Take the prescribed quantity of water, sand and cement and mix carefully until you end up with a homogenous mixture that is of the right consistency and is ready for use. If you lack the patience, you can use quick-setting cement, but then you run the risk of everything drying too quickly and you having to rush.

2 Fill a plastic mould with potting compost. For best results, use a coarse compost. Model the potting compost into a dish shape. When you are happy with the shape, add a layer of cement over the surface. Do not spread too thinly otherwise the dish will break at a later stage. Press the cement firmly into the compost, so that the outside of the dish is covered in compost.

3 Do the same with the inside of the dish. Fill it up with compost so as not to lose the shape. When it is dry, carefully remove the dish from the mould. Do not clean it up, but simply tap off excess turf for the right look.

4 Start planting up at one side and work your way to the other side. For this, do not use soil but peat moss. Plant up the first third with *Equisetum*, then orchids and then another batch of *Equisetum*. To finish off the natural look, add a few pieces of wood covered in moss to the dish.

Bird's nest

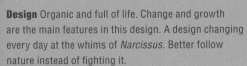

Designer
Per
Materials
Narcissus 'Tête-à-tête'
Salix / willow
bullion wire
dry foam
eggs
feathers
Mizuhiki wire
plant soil

Design Organic and full of life. Change and growth are the main features in this design. A design changing every day at the whims of *Narcissus*. Better follow nature instead of fighting it.
Technique Arranging technique. In this design, we do not plant anything, which allows easy maintenance and changing the flowers. Gluing and binding techniques are used for the eggs and feathers. No water is needed, the *Narcissus* have all they need in their bulbs.
Emotions Life and beginning life. Flowers growing out of eggs in a nest announce spring and Easter. New life is born and changes every day.

1 For this arrangement we need both fully grown and budding *Narcissus*. This for the feel, shape and movement of the arrangement. Wash away all soil from the bulbs and let them dry well.

2 Use bullion thread to wire feathers onto Mizuhiki wire. Make or buy ready made eggs of different colours and materials. Wire dry grass and moss onto Styrofoam eggs, and glue willow catkins and leaves on others.

3 Place the *Narcissus* inside the eggs. When needed, use glue to stabilize. Do this in advance, so that the Narcissus have grown towards the light and show beautiful curves.

4 Arrange moss into the container and place the different eggs inside, creating an organized mess. Finish the arrangement with the Mizuhiki wire and feathers, and make sure to follow the beautiful curves of the *Narcissus*. 81

Flowering porcelain

Designer
Tomas
Materials
Carex (sedges)
Ficus pumila (creeping fig)
Phalaenopsis (butterfly orchid)
Mitsumata twigs *(Edgeworthia chrysantha)*
Clay pellets
Potting compost
Two china dishes

Design The power of the colour white is central. White stands for purity, righteousness, neutrality, innocence, … values which this arrangement exudes and which are reinforced by the choice of plants, including *Phalaenopsis* and grasses. An ostensibly simple design that can be displayed on its own in an open and modern interior.
Technique A relatively simple and pleasing design. Place two unique, hand-made porcelain dishes on top of each other to create another base shape. Divide the Mitsumata twigs evenly across the arrangement and secure firmly in the soil. *Ficus pumila* adds a playful touch and breaks up the linear movement.
Emotions Transparency, fragility and innocence are words which this arrangement evokes. Purity that transcends egos and brings us closer to the truth.

1 Two porcelain bowls as the basis, a few Mitsumata twigs to help define shape, *Phalaenopsis* as the main plant and *Carex* and Ficus *pumila* as additional green ingredients. The combination of green and white sets the tone of this arrangement.

2 Before planting up, place a layer of clay pellets at the bottom of the dish. Next, plant up the *Phalaenopsis* and the other plants. Leave some room between the plants for the Mitsumata twigs.

3 Plant up closely together, but leave room for a few aerial roots of the *Phalaenopsis*. Allow the *Ficus pumila* to hang over the rim of the bowls to break up the rigidity of the piece.

4 Finish off with the Mitsumata twigs and more soil. Make sure the twigs are distributed evenly but avoid symmetry. The twigs can be used to support the orchid flowers.

83

Transition

Designer
Max
Materials
Convallaria majalis (Lily of the Valley)
Fritillaria meleagris
Prunus
Sphagnum (peat moss)
Container
Clay pellets
Potting compost

Design A fully planted-up container that can hold its own. The lines of the dish are used and echoed, anything exceeding these are trimmed. A decorative, yet clearly delineated design.

Technique By starting off with a layer of clay pellets, we can reduce the risk of the plant roots being constantly wet. Any excess water at the top will be stored by the peat moss which also reduces the risk of the plant drying out. Make sure all the roots make good contact with the potting compost.

Emotion The purity of spring is translated into materials and colours. The force of spring is demonstrated by the shape. The promise of yet more beauty to come is concealed in the design.

1 Half-fill the container with clay pellets so that any excess water can be drained off. Add a layer of potting compost.

2 Carefully remove the plants from their pots, making sure the roots are not damaged in the process. The *Prunus* is divided up equally in the pot. Branches that overhang the shape can be trimmed. When planting, also consider the natural shape and direction of growth.

3 Plant the *Fritillaria* and Lily-of-the-Valley randomly in amongst the *Prunus*. Make sure you do not plant them all from the side but also from the centre and through the *Prunus* for an attractive, even growing style.

4 Cover the potting compost with *Sphagnum*, ensuring that no peat moss overhangs the edges, for this will absorb all the water from the pot. Anything overhanging the edges must be trimmed. Water freely.

Garden kitsch

Designer
Per
Materials
Phormium
canna sticks
clay granules (L.E.C.A)
container
glue gun
plant soil
plastic foam sheets
zip ties

1 For this plant arrangement we use both botanical and artificial materials to create a strong expression of lines, shapes and colours. Use well watered plants and trim off any dead ends on the *Phormium* leaves.

2 Cut squares from coloured soft plastic. These will be used both on the container as on the decorative top part of the arrangement.

3 Use any kind of odd, unwanted container, but clean it well. Glue on big sheets of soft plastic to cover the entire surface of the container. The smaller plastic squares are glued on in an irregular flowing pattern, but with most squares directed to the top of the container.

4 When planted, start pushing in the coloured canna sticks following the shape of the container. Attach zip ties to some of the leaves and pierce on soft plastic squares. A final touch, connecting the bottom and top of this arrangement.

Design A plant arrangement where colour and geometric lines and shapes are the main focus. The former inspired by the bold colour of the *Phormium*, the latter by the direction and the shape of the leaves.
Technique Allow a good layer of clay granules in the container to allow water storage. Gluing, zip-tying and piercing techniques. Always trim your plants, cut away dead ends and clean all parts before use.
Emotions Is this real or not? Bring kitsch and nature together in a soft, colourful way, not a screaming for attention kind of way. Our florist's decorative knowledge goes beyond the home interior and is used outdoor on terraces and in gardens.

Colourful loops

Designer
Max
Materials
Celosia argentea / cockscomb
Potting compost
Pink ornamental stones or broken glass
Dish

1 Fill one side of the dish with potting compost mixed with plant food. For practical reasons, do not fill up the dish completely with potting compost at this stage.

2 Select and sort plants according to size and colour and remove any damaged leaves. Give the plants a good soak in a basin filled with water before arranging them according to colour. Determine the mutual distance by planting a first line across the middle of the dish.

3 Work your way around the dish in circles, whilst adding potting compost from the side. Make sure the root system is in firm contact with the soil and that the distance between the plants is always the same.

4 Once the dish has been planted up completely, water the plants and clean up the dish. Make sure the potting compost has been skimmed to give an even surface, but ensure that a watering channel is left. Finish off with a thick layer of coloured ornamental stones to bring out the colour.

Design A colourful, ornamental dish to brighten up the patio. By planting up the material in circles, the round shape of the dish is accentuated.
Technique It is important to give the plants a good soak before planting up. Use the right potting compost and make sure that the roots are in close contact with the potting compost.
Emotions A colourful dish for the patio. The bright colours and loops add an instant splash of sun an warmth. Positive summery emotions.

Unity

Designer
Tomas
Materials
Azalea indica 'Sachsenstern'
Sphagnum (peat moss)
Wooden plant sticks
Metal container
Plastic sphere (90cm diameter)

Design An impressive, geometric creation. The sphere is the focal point of this design. By placing this plant arrangement in a certain environment or against a background, you end up with a surprising composition.
Technique A large plastic sphere with holes the size of azalea clumps is the core component for this plant arrangement. The peat moss provides the azaleas with sufficient water so that they can continue to grow in and on the sphere. A respectful technique which maximises the longevity of the arrangement.
Emotion Much like a drop of water forms part of the ocean, so do the circles, the azalea sphere and bamboo form a unity. The wave-like motion in the jungle of bamboo stands for energy, while the water stored in the peat moss is the source of life.

1 Use a sphere (90cm diameter) with as many holes as possible, each one the pot size of the azaleas. Distribute the holes as evenly as possible. To support the sphere and to be able to place it at a height, you will also need a suitable support structure.

2 Before placing the azaleas into the sphere, submerge them until their clumps no longer produce any air bubbles. This is when the clumps are completely saturated. Place the azaleas in the sphere, starting at the bottom. Place them in the holes and insert a plant stick through the roots so that the plants cannot drop out of the sphere. Fill the core of the sphere with saturated *Sphagnum*. The moss will provide the plants with plenty of water.

3 Work your way up and continue to fill the core with moss. Plant up the last azalea loosely in the design, making sure each time it is surrounded by the wet moss and the round shape of the sphere is kept.

4 Where the sphere threatens to lose its shape, press the plants deeper or trim away some of the wayward sprigs. Moisten the sphere one last time, so that all the *Sphagnum* is completely saturated and place the design in the desired environment.

91

1

2

3

4

Ornamental simplicity

Designer
Max
Materials
Begonia tenella (80)
Wire mesh (with mesh openings of 15x15cm)
Moss
Potting compost
Tendrils
Wooden sticks

1 Fill the vase to the rim with potting compost and press down firmly. Make a column using wire mesh with a diameter that is 10cm smaller than the diameter of the pot.

2 Use sticks to secure the wire mesh in the pot. Give the *Begonias* a good soak before using them. Squeeze the side of the pot to dislodge the plants without damaging the roots.

3 Plant the *Begonias* upwards in a spiral movement. Moss ensures that the soil is kept in place. Work very carefully for a fine finish. After every circle, add more compost in the middle and press down carefully to ensure contact with the root system.

4 Finally, drape the tendrils over the arrangement, add compost and press it down firmly. Check whether the moss is attached firmly and repair or reinforce where necessary. After a while, the root system of the *Begonias* will be sufficiently developed to keep everything in place.

Design A traditional arrangement using just one plant species. The strong *Begonia* is eminently suited for this arrangement: the *Begonia* will survive temporary drought without any problems and the arrangement will retain its shape for a few months at least.
Technique Follow the instructions carefully. Make sure the compost is pressed down firmly so that the plants can settle in properly and use the moss with care so that the compost does not spill out from the arrangement.
Emotion The strong shape combined with the same species of white *Begonias* lends the arrangement serenity and dignity and is very decorative.

93

Spiraled

Designer
Per
Materials
Kalanchoe
aluminium wire
floral foam (large ball or bricks)
glue gun
plant soil
wax

Design A decorative, round plant arrangement using only one type of flower. Sometimes it is better, both for the life and the maintenance of the plant as well as for aesthetics, to work creatively with accents. A simple base with an abundance of decoration.
Technique Planting, dripping and piercing in and on dry foam. Plant with respect, trim foliage and make sure the container is waterproof. When pushing in the decorative spirals, do not let them pierce completely through the container. The spirals on top are pushed into the soil from above. Make sure you do not damage the plants when doing so.
Emotions Who can stop smiling when seeing this plant arrangement? Play on people's emotions when creating. Whether it's a smile from like or dislike isn't as important as generating attention and reactions.

1 Trim off most of the foliage from the *Kalanchoe* to minimize the green in this arrangement. Use plants that show a lot of colour.

2 To make the actual container, either use the biggest floral foam ball that is sold or carve a sphere from stacked floral foam bricks. Carve out the centre quite deep to give the plants space and sufficient soil. If you build your own ball shape, use hot glue and fill in all the gaps in between the bricks to waterproof it.

3 Melt wax in a color matching the arrangement and pour it over the dry foam, both from top to bottom and from bottom to top, in order to cover the entire surface. Do this layer after layer, make sure each layer has enough time to dry and continue until no more foam is visible.

4 Make lots of different sized aluminium spirals for decorative use. Start at the centre with a longer 'handle', this will keep the circles in place when pushed into the foam container, and work your way out until you reach a spiral of the desired size. Do think of dominance in colours and sizes.

5 The wax coated structure is now covered in aluminium spirals. Place and group them according to colour and add some over the edge of the container, to connect the base and the plant part of this design.

Creations & step-by-step instructions
Per Benjamin (SE)
Tomas De Bruyne (BE)
Max van de Sluis (NL)

History & Future text
Per Benjamin (SE)

Drawings
Kathy van de Sluis-Kim (NL)

Photography
Kurt Dekeyzer (BE)
Helén Pe (SE)
Pim van der Maden (NL)
Dirk Wullus (BE)

Translation
Taal-Ad-Visie, Brugge (BE)

Final Editing
Katrien Van Moerbeke

Layout
www.groupvandamme.eu

Print
www.pureprint.be

Published by
Stichting Kunstboek bvba
Legeweg 165
B-8020 Oostkamp
Belgium
tel. +32 50 46 19 10
fax +32 50 46 19 18
info@stichtingkunstboek.com
www.stichtingkunstboek.com

ISBN 978-90-5856-352-1
D/2011/6407/02
NUR 421

Per

Max

Tomas

life³

a bundle of creativity www.life3.net

Life3 is an international partnership consisting of Per Benjamin, Max van de Sluis and Tomas De Bruyne. Per started working with flowers at an early age, almost by accident, and now has his own consulting companies, Benjamins Botaniska in Stockholm. Tomas is a floral designer who brightens up events and happenings worldwide. He has a consulting company in Belgium and is an internationally established value.

They have all worked in various fields of the flower industry, ranging from nurseries, wholesalers and retail shops, and each of them is devoted to both commercial and artistic designs focusing on the emotional side of flowers. Per, Max and Tomas value the importance of training and give demonstrations and classes all around the world as well as in their home countries.

Per, Max and Tomas have taken part in many competitions and have won several medals both nationally and internationally. At the 2002 World Cup in the Netherlands they were first, third and fifth (respectively Per, Max and Tomas). In the aftermath of the competition, they ended up talking and commenting on each other's works. Once they got talking, they started playing with the idea of working together in the future. It soon became clear that they shared the same ideas and visions. Only half a year later, Life3 was born.

Life3 stands for emotions, creativity, craftsmanship and communication. This partnership, the first of its kind between three florists, aims to add new value to the flower industry. It wants to take floral design up to new levels and wishes to bring it to a wider audience. Life3 offers demonstrations, workshops, decorations, shows, seminars and books — both educational and purely inspirational — and education for small and big groups. They offer trend information, product design and development, everything within the world of flowers and beyond.